Thanks!

Gumballs
Little Treats to Chew On

words by Brian Addison | pictures by Zac Rybacki

To our families.

Proudly self-published by Gumballs Books
Printed and bound in the U.S.A. by Signature Book Printing

ISBN 978-0-615-73781-2

We're so happy that you have this book.
We hope you're excited to give it a look.
Get ready, get set, then fill in the blanks.
Re-using is good, the earth will say "Thanks."

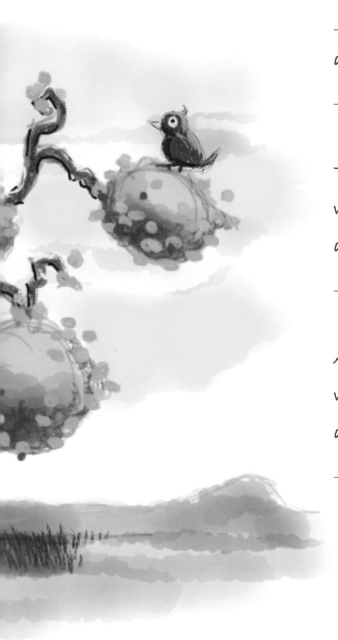

At first, this book was the property of
_____, who read it with _____
and _____ and sometimes
_____.

Then it was passed along to _____,
who laughed about it with _____
and _____, and yes, even
_____.

And then it fell in the hands of _____,
who learned from it with _____
and _____, and believe it or not,
_____ !

Enter

Be filled with hope,
Ye who enter here.
For this space is a place
Of smiles and cheer.

Ideas 'round each corner,
Surprises each turn.
Questions to ask,
And lessons to learn.

So be you old, or be you young,
or be you in between.
May you leave looking to share
all that you have seen.

Fridge of Gold

I saw something cool at the refrigerator store.
A 10 foot high fridge with big shiny doors.

It made ice cubes all by itself
In the ice cube tray on the ice cube shelf.

It wrapped up your chicken, it seasoned your steaks.
It made eggs and toast and butterscotch shakes.

It threw the milk out when the milk went bad.
It cheered up the kitchen when the kitchen was sad.

It danced, it sang, it told the time.
It told jokes to the lemons that lived with the limes.

What a treasure it was, this fridge of gold.
Did everything right but keep the food cold.

Tommy Tongue Twister

Tommy Tongue Twister
Could say everything well.
From "thick thimbles on thumbs"
To "Sally's seashells."

He could speak the "sixth sheik,"
Blurt "rubber baby buggy bumpers."
Could say 1,000 times fast,
"Dump trucks struck truckers' dumpers."

But there was one twister he just couldn't say
No matter how hard Tommy tried.
That was the day Tommy Tongue Twister
Became Tommy Tongue Tied.

Monsters

Think about all the monsters
You see when you dream.
The ones you can't escape,
The ones that make you scream.

They get tired from chasing you
And being up late at night.
They have a lot of children to scare,
The schedule they run is tight.

Whenever they get a chance,
They try to get some rest.
As soon as they go to sleep
It's your turn to be the pest.

Go holler and jump upon their heads
While they lay in their monster beds.
Tell them "leave me alone you ogres and beasts!"
"I won't be a part of your kid-eating feasts."

A lesson they'll learn and learn very fast,
That if they scare you, you'll surely laugh last.

Land of Baleens

Whenever you lose something of yours,
You look under tables and inside your drawers.
In every last corner of every last place,
"My things have vanished to outer space!"

You're very close if that's where you guessed.
It's near outer space, just ten miles west.
A place never heard of, a world never seen.
All lost is found in the land of Baleens.

They're short and friendly, no Baleen's ever mean.
They have large round noses, and hair that's bright green.
Whatever you've lost is found in their homes.
Misplaced things fill the world of these giggling gnomes.

Keys everywhere for doors they don't know.
Puppies and kittens running to and fro.
76 remotes for every TV.
Phone numbers for all from A to Z.

A baseball you lost in the yard next door,
Baleen Bob just threw to Baleen Theodore.
So take care of this poem, know where it is at all times.
The Baleens have a lot, but they don't have these rhymes!

Fubby Gringers

Wash your hands before you eat.
Yeah those same hands that scraped your feet.

The same ten fingers that probed your nose,
Got rid of the jam between your toes.

What was that goop all over your finger?
Remember that smell? And wow did it linger!

Would you eat a sandwich made of that?
Might as well add the fur from your cat.

Get rid of those germs and worms and slime,
Just use soap and water before dinner time!

Tooth Fairy

What a busy night!
First I'll go visit Ruth,
The eight-year-old girl
With an extra loose tooth.

Almost gone from her mouth,
Hanging just by a thread.
I'll snag that fang
From under her head!

Business for me
Is such a thrill.
Get one baby tooth,
Leave one dollar bill.

Where do these teeth go?
Do I stick them in piles?
They go back to my shop
Where they're made into smiles.

Then I hit the street
Selling door to door.
Looking for sad people
Who should be smiling more.

I'll sell them a grin,
Get them happy for cheap.
And leave a bit for you later,
You won't hear a peep.

Mouth and Ear

The mouth showed up for class today,
And like always had a lot to say.
It talked, and rambled, and gabbed away.
It might not yet be done.

The ear was in the class next door,
With the sleeping nose that liked to snore.
It spoke far less, but listened more.
And for that was the wiser one.

My Biggest Lunch

Wait until you hear what I had for lunch.
Why have one thing when you can have a bunch?

I had a BUN, a PEAR, some JAM and TEA,
A PIE, and RICE topped with a NUT and a PEA.

Then a PEN, and a HAT, and a CAR, and a FAN,
And a PIG with a BAG, and an OX in a CAN.

Slurped it right down, spelled every word I could see.
Left only two letters, ate YOU but not ME.

Gumballs

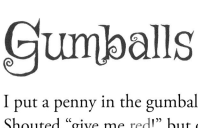

I put a penny in the gumball machine.
Shouted "give me red!" but out came green.

Another penny in, another gumball out.
This one would be red, I had no doubt.

Boo-hoo, boo-hoo! The next one was blue.
That left only one thing for me to do.

50 pennies later I had aquamarine,
Chartreuse, taupe and colors never seen.

"I want red, I want red!"
"Not every color instead!"

I begged, pleaded, got down on my knees,
And finally realized I never said "please."

Different

Wouldn't it be great if we all were the same?
With identical clothes and only one name?

Hey you like chocolate? Wow I do too!
But I don't like opera at all, do you?

We would have so much fun if we all were alike.
You wanna go play? Hey, I have that bike!

And that toy and that hat and that baseball card.
And that same tree house in my backyard.

But wait a minute, there's something wrong,
If we all were the same, would we all get along?

Would we if we had the same dreams and emotions?
Or miss all the good that can come from commotion?

We'd never learn about anything new,
If we only picked red but never picked blue.

The lesson here is that different is good.
So if you're feeling different, remember, you should.

A lifelong Chicagoan, Brian Addison loves throwing dance parties with his wife and two children. He's spent his career as a marketing and advertising guy.

Brian graduated from Northwestern University with an economics degree, and returned a few years later for his MBA from the Kellogg School of Management.

Zac Rybacki is a husband and father living in the Chicago area. He enjoys drawing, playing the accordion, and for a living works as a creative director.

Zac was born and raised in the Milwaukee area and has a fine arts degree from the Milwaukee Institute of Art & Design.

How many times have you read this book?
Well here's one way to gauge.
Color one gumball each time you read it,
and this page will get better with age!

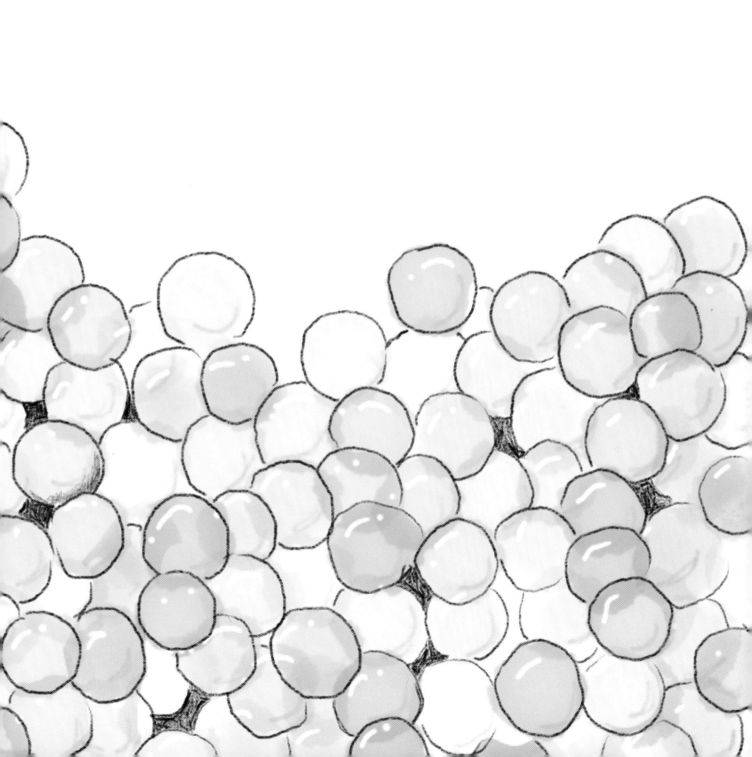